MW00440782

Easy Slow Cooker Crock Pot Recipes

Robertina Whelans

Ordinary Matters Publishing

All Rights Reserved

DASH DIET EASY SLOW COOKER CROCK POT RECIPES
Ordinary Matters Publishing
Ordinary MattersPublishing.com

DISCLAIMER: The recipes within this book, DASH DIET Easy Slow Cooker Crock Pot Recipes, are for information purposes only and are not meant as a diet to treat, prescribe, or diagnose illness. Please seek the advice of a doctor or alternative health care professional if you have any health issues you would like addressed or before you begin any diet.

Book Layout © 2014 BookDesignTemplates.com

DASH DIET Easy Slow Cooker Crock Pot Recipes / Robertina Whelans-1st Ed.
ASIN: BOOKSNES7K (eBook - 2014)
ISBN—10: 1-941303-58-7 (print)
ISBN—13: 978-1-941303-58-0 (print)

https://www.amazon.com/author/dashdiet

www.facebook.com/DASH-Diet-Smoothies-and-Recipes

*"Your diet is a bank account.
Good food choices are good investments."*

—BETHANY FRANKEL

CONTENTS

INTRODUCTION

If you've ever experienced high blood pressure (hypertension), then you know it can be debilitating. Apparently, most people don't have any symptoms. Not so with me. I woke up one day with a terrible headache and it lasted for days. I also noticed that I had swelling in my lower legs and feet. A friend suggested I get a blood pressure monitor. To be honest, I didn't expect much. Most of the time my blood pressure was normal, but there would be times when it would run low; so you can imagine my surprise when the readings revealed that my blood pressure had sky-rocketed.

A quick trip to the doctor and a prescription soon had my blood pressure under control. By then, I had started on a campaign to learn all I could about hypertension. I discovered that high blood pressure could lead to more severe problems like heart disease and even kidney disease. I wanted to know what I could do to reduce my blood pressure and keep it lowered without having to take daily medication. That's when I came across the DASH Diet.

I immediately began to apply the principles of the DASH Diet and changed my eating habits. My blood pressure dropped and the need for the medicine decreased. Not only was I able to stop taking the daily blood pressure pill, I lost weight.

Because of my own experience, I wanted to share the benefits of the DASH Diet with others by putting together a series of DASH Diet cookbook.

What is the DASH Diet?

The DASH diet is a simple, effective, and scientifically-proven diet that produces results. For more than twenty years, physicians have suggested this diet for their patients who have hypertension (high blood pressure). Today, studies show that the DASH diet is effective in helping those who have high cholesterol and those who have elevated blood sugar levels and either are diabetic or are prone to the disease.

Because studies have shown that the DASH diet lowers bad cholesterol levels, doctors also prescribe the diet for their heart patients. Now we know the diet is an effect weight-loss program, too. Every day, more and more is revealed about the value and benefits of the Dash diet. Even Doctor Oz. has done several shows on the merits of DASH.

The DASH diet stands for "Dietary Approaches to Stop Hypertension." Originally developed by the US National Institute of Health, as a way to lower blood pressure without medication, it is now ranked as one of the healthiest diets around, and has achieved the title "Best diet for diabetes," four years in a row.

Known also as the "diet for all diseases," it has been proven to improve health over a variety of different conditions.

By following the dietary advice within the DASH diet, it is possible to reduce your blood pressure by a few points in as little as two weeks. Prolonged use of the diet can see systolic blood pressure reduce by anything up to 12 points, which is significant in treating high blood pressure and its resultant effects.

Lowered risk of heart disease, stroke, cholesterol, kidney failure, and several types of cancer are all benefits of the DASH diet. More so, with its emphasis on real foods, especially fruits and vegetables, and the right amount of protein, the DASH diet has proven itself to be a great weight loss tool.

The diet is high in potassium, calcium, and magnesium, all minerals that help reduce high blood pressure. It is also low in sodium, which has been proven to increase blood pressure.

Incorporating the DASH diet with the principles of slow cooking actually works really well.

Undoubtedly the biggest benefit of slow cooking is the time element. Saving time on preparing food is probably a women's biggest concern, as she rushes around working, juggling childcare, and trying to provide her family with great food.

Following the DASH diet will see you eating plenty of flavorsome whole foods, and it is here that slow cooking has other benefits. Cooking food slowly locks in the flavor, as cooking liquids don't evaporate as they do in the oven. So, food cooked in the slow cooker keeps its flavor, and in many cases has the flavor enhanced, which is a great bonus seeing as you will be eating lots of lovely healthy vegetables and cuts of meat.

Incorporating the principles of the DASH diet should be a lifestyle practice, and not just a short-term solution to health problems or weight loss. Anything that helps you stick to the diet so that you can start to see the benefits is a useful tool to have, and slow cooking should certainly be one of your tools.

DASH Diet Guidelines

Food Group	Serving	Serving size
Grains	6 - 8	½ cup of cooked rice or pasta.
Fruits	4 – 5	2 cups
Vegetables	4 – 5	2 cups
Protein	3 or less	1 cup tofu, tempeh or seitan
Fats and Oils	2 – 3	1 tbsp.
Sweets and added sugar	5 or less per week	-

Slow Cooking

The DASH diet is perfect for anyone who loves slow-cooking methods. As far as I'm concerned a Crock-Pot, or slow cooker as it's often called these days, is a wonderful kitchen tool and a terrific way to cook. I remember getting my first Crock Pot in the early 1970s. I loved it, probably for all the reasons you do today. Let's face it, nothing unlocks flavors like the cook low, cook slow method.

In this collection of recipes, you'll find a wide range of slow cooker recipes that work for the DASH diet. There are recipes that call for chicken, beef, and pork, as well as vegetarian dishes.

The History of the Modern Slow Cooker

Let me just say that slow cooking is not a modern phenomena. There is evidence that clay pots were used over wood fires going back some six thousand years. We may not have any ancient recipes, but the cooking method is as useful today as it was necessary then.

Prior to the 70s many cooks relied on appliances like the electric bean pot, a simple ceramic pot that had a heating element that allowed you to cook beans all day, instead of using the stovetop.

The original modern crock pot was invented by Irving Naxon who received his patent in January 1940, and forever changed the landscape of home cooking. His Lithuanian grandmother was the inspiration for Nixon's slow cooker invention, when he learned of a dish of hers called Cholent that would be cooked overnight. His grandmother would take her pot of ingredients to the local bakery and use their oven. Naxon came up with the idea of using that "low and slow" method by putting the crock inside a heating unit. The cooks of the 1950s loved the idea.

The first big wave came in 1970 when Rival Mfg. bought Naxon's idea and produced the first, original "Crock-Pot." This classic appliance came in several colors of the day and even had its own cookbook. You'll find the classic pot roast as well as stews, chili, and curry. Want a good soup or a slow-cooked dessert? No problem. You'll find these slow cooker recipes to be a wonderful addition to your cookbook collection.

Why Are Slow Cookers So Popular?

Convenience and flavorful cooking are the two main reasons modern cooks have embraced slow cookers. The original Crock-Pot hit the market at a time when women were entering the workforce in a major way. Slow cooking made it easy for a working mom to feed her family a delicious hot dinner at the end of a long work day. It seemed almost effortless.

In 1975 more than three million Crock-Pots found their way into homes. Even in the early 2000s, it was discovered that more than eighty percent of homes in the United States still owned a slow cooker. Why not? They are easy and definitely energy efficient.

Slow Cookers Today

Today slow cookers have come into their own. They are easy to use, easy to clean. The crock part is removable so portability has increased. If you have a slow cooker with a rubber seal and a lock, they make it easy to carry the food from one place to another. Some can even stir themselves and others come with automatic timers and temperature probes. Would you believe you can even buy one with a built-in Wi-Fi.

Benefits of Slow Cooker Cooking

There are a three big reasons why today's cooks turn to slow cookers to prepare meals.

1. Easy clean-up
2. Ability to use less expensive meats
3. Convenient

What to Cook in a Slow Cooker

Slow cookers are used to create a wide variety of dishes from soup and beans, to stews, meat, and seafood, as well as vegetable dishes and desserts. Pot roasts are a staple. Families enjoy classic dishes like pot pies, chilies, stews, curries, and beans. It would seem you can pretty much slow cook anything you can imagine.

Slow Cooking Tips

Here are twelve things to keep in mind when you use a slow cooker.

Monitor your slow cooker when you first start using it on high and on low. You don't want to go away for hours only to return and find out the new cooker has a problem overheating.

Completely thaw frozen food before adding it to the slow cooker. Unless the frozen items are specifically created for slow cooker meals, you will increase the possibility for bacteria to grow.

Place your slow cooker on some kind of surface like a baking sheet, stovetop, or granite countertop because it does get hot.

Don't lift the lid to check on the food. You will only add more cooking time.

Don't stir the food. That will add more time to the cooking process.

For full flavor, brown the meat, especially ground meat. You can also sauté the vegetables before putting them into the slow cooker. If you use flour to cover the meat before browning, you'll get a much thicker sauce.

Take advantage of layering, but make sure you put firm vegetables like potatoes and carrots on the bottom, and then add the meat. You'll get better results if everything is cut up in equal sizes, too.

Wait to add any dairy products like yogurt, milk, or sour cream. Add them about fifteen minutes before you're ready to serve.

Cut the fat and the chicken skin. You don't want that oily, greasy taste.

Additional Notes

_____

_____

_____

_____

_____

_____

_____

_____

_____

_____

_____

_____

_____

_____

_____

CHICKEN RECIPES

Chicken and Rice Stew

Servings: 6

Ingredients:
2 medium carrots, peeled and sliced
2 medium leeks, trimmed and sliced
½ onion, chopped
1 cup uncooked, brown rice
12 oz. boneless, skinless chicken, chopped into small pieces
1 tsp. thyme
½ tsp. rosemary
36 oz. chicken stock
1 x 10 oz. can mushroom soup
1 clove garlic
Sea salt and pepper to season

Instructions:
Place carrots, onion, leeks, rice, and garlic into your slow cooker.

Add chicken, thyme, rosemary and season with the salt and pepper.

Pour in the chicken stock and soup. Stir, making sure it is mixed well.

Place lid on and cook on low-heat setting for about 7-8 hours, or on the high-heat setting for 3 ½ — 4 hours.

Serve immediately, or leave on the warm setting until needed.

Nutritional Information: (per serving)
Calories 245
Total Fat 6.2g
Saturated Fat 1.6g
Cholesterol 35.1mg
Sodium 1761mg
Total Carbs 21g
Dietary Fiber 1.5g
Sugar 2.2g
Protein 25.2g

_____

_____

_____

_____

_____

_____

Salsa Chicken

Servings: 6

Ingredients:
32 oz. chicken breasts, skinless and chopped into pieces
1 cup salsa (low sodium)
1 cup diced, canned tomatoes (low sodium)
2 tbsp. taco seasoning
1 cup onions, finely chopped
½ cup celery, finely chopped
½ cup carrots, shredded
3 tbsp. sour cream, reduced fat

Instructions:
Place the chicken in the bottom of the slow cooker.

Sprinkle the taco seasoning over the top, and then layer the vegetables, and the salsa on top of that.

Pour half a cup of water over the layers, and set the cooker on the low-heat setting for 6 – 8 hours.

When ready to serve, stir the chicken and vegetables together, and mix in the sour cream.

Serve on its own or with rice or potatoes.

Nutritional Information: (per serving - does not include rice or potatoes)

Calories 165
Total Fat 2.5g
Saturated Fat 0.8g
Cholesterol 67.9mg
Sodium 253.3mg
Total Carbs 7.3g
Dietary Fiber 2.1g
Sugar 1.5g
Protein 27.6g

_____

_____

_____

_____

_____

_____

_____

_____

_____

Provencal Chicken and Vegetables

Servings: 6

Ingredients:
24 oz. chicken, skinless, boneless, and chopped into pieces
1 yellow bell pepper, sliced
1 red bell pepper, sliced
1 x 16 oz. cannellini beans, drained and rinsed
1 x 14 oz. can diced, tomatoes (low sodium)
2 tsp. dried basil
1 tsp. dried thyme
Sea salt and pepper to season

Instructions:
Add all the ingredients to the slow cooker and stir, mixing together well.

Cover with lid, and cook on the low heat setting for 7 hours.

Serve immediately or leave on warm setting. The dish will last for up to 8 hours on a warm setting, and the flavors will really infuse.

Nutritional Information: (per serving)
Calories 225kcal

Total Fat 3.2g

Saturated Fat 0.8g

Cholesterol 70.2mg

Sodium 829mg

Total Carbs 19.8g

Dietary Fiber 4.9g

Sugar 5.5g

Protein 29.7g

_____

_____

_____

_____

_____

_____

_____

_____

_____

Lemony Garlic Chicken

Servings: 6

Ingredients:
6 chicken breasts, skinless
1 tbsp. extra virgin olive oil
¼ cup water
3 tbsp. lemon juice
1 tsp. dried oregano
2 tsp. minced garlic
1 tsp. chicken stock granules
1 tsp. dried parsley
¼ tsp. black pepper
Sea salt to season

Instructions:
Mix the oregano and black pepper together, and rub evenly over the chicken breasts.

In a large frying pan, gently brown the chicken on both sides.

Place the chicken in the slow cooker, and add the other ingredients.

Cover with the lid, and cook on the low heat setting for 6 hours, or the high heat setting for 3 hours.

Serve immediately with brown rice or other vegetables, or leave on the warm setting until required.

Nutritional Information: (per serving - not including rice or other vegetables)

Calories 167kcal
Total Fat 5.6g
Saturated Fat 1.2g
Cholesterol 73mg
Sodium 128mg
Total Carbs 1g
Dietary Fiber 0.2g
Sugar 0g
Protein 27g

Additional Notes

Use this section to make additional notes.

_____

_____

_____

_____

_____

_____

_____

_____

_____

_____

_____

_____

_____

_____

BEEF RECIPES

Lasagna

Servings: 8

Ingredients:
16 oz. lean (96%) ground beef
¼ tsp. red pepper flakes
2 tsp. dried thyme
24 oz. jar marinara sauce (low sodium)
1 eggplant, chopped
15 oz. ricotta cheese, low fat
1 cup shredded hard cheese
1 egg white
1 tbsp. fresh parsley
6 no-boil lasagna sheets

Instructions:
In a pan, brown the ground beef, and drain any fat.

Stir in the pepper flakes, thyme, marinara sauce, eggplant, and 1 ¼ cups water.

In a separate bowl, mix the egg white, ricotta, shredded cheese, and parsley until well mixed.

Coat the inside of the slow cooker with oil. Cover the bottom of the cooker with a layer of the meat sauce. Top with two or three of the lasagna sheets.

Add another layer of meat sauce, and 2-3 more of the lasagna sheets.

Add the cheese sauce, and finish off with another layer of meat sauce.

Set the cooker on a low heat setting, and cook for 3 ½ to 4 hours. No more. (Do not overcook.)

Note, that this recipe is not an all-day recipe and will not do well from being kept warm. Once it is cooked, you will need to eat it immediately.

Nutritional Information:

Calories 271
Total Fat 10.2g
Saturated Fat 5.6g
Cholesterol 56.5mg
Sodium 284mg
Total Carbs 18g
Dietary Fiber 1.6g
Sugar 3.2g
Protein 25g

Beef and Mushrooms

Servings: 4

16 oz. lean ground beef (96%)

1 x 10 oz. can low-fat cream of mushroom soup

½ cup water

1 onion, chopped

1 tbsp. beef stock granules

8 oz. fresh mushrooms

Ingredients:

Add the meat to a pan and brown.

Place meat in the slow cooker. Add mushrooms on top.

Mix the soup, water, and beef granules together, and then pour over the beef and mushrooms.

Cook on a low heat setting for 6-8 hours, or the high heat setting for 3-4 hours.

Keep warm if not using immediately.

This dish can be served with rice and/or other vegetables.

Instructions:

Nutritional Information: per serving - not including rice or other vegetables

Calories 214
Total Fat 6g
Saturated Fat 2.1g
Cholesterol 71.2mg
Sodium 976mg
Total Carbs 12.4g
Dietary Fiber 1.7g
Sugar 2.6g
Protein 27g

_____

_____

_____

_____

_____

_____

_____

_____

_____

Beef Roast and Vegetables

Servings: 6

Ingredients:
40 oz. beef roast, English or Cross Rib cut
5 red skin, new potatoes, washed and quartered
1 large parsnip, peeled and sliced
1 ½ cups baby carrots, peeled
1 onion, chopped
1 rutabaga, peeled and sliced
1 tsp. black pepper
½ tsp. sea salt
1 tbsp. all-purpose flour
1 x 14 oz. can diced tomatoes (low-sodium)
1 tsp. dried thyme
1 bay leaf, whole

Instructions:
Place all vegetables in the bottom of the slow cooker.

Season both sides of the meat with salt and pepper.

Pre-heat a large pan, lightly flour the meat, and seer it on all sides for about 3-4 minutes per side.

Place the meat on top of the vegetables.

Mix the tomato sauce and the rest of the seasonings together.

Pour over the meat and cook on the low heat setting for 8-9 hours.

Serve immediately, or leave on the warm setting until required.

Nutritional Information: per serving
Calories 350
Total Fat 9.3g
Saturated Fat 3.1g
Cholesterol 111mg
Sodium 342mg
Total Carbs 21g
Dietary Fiber 4.2g
Sugar 4.8g
Protein 44g

Moroccan Beef Stew

Servings: 8

Ingredients:
32 oz. lean beef, cut into small pieces
4 carrots, peeled and sliced
2 medium onions, peeled and sliced
3 cloves garlic
1 tsp. curry powder
¼ cup tomato puree
24 oz. beef broth (low sodium)
1 x 14.5 oz. can chickpeas, drained and rinsed
½ cup raisins
½ cup chopped apricots
2 tbsp. chopped cilantro (coriander)
¼ cup almond slices

Instructions:

Dry the meat with a paper towel.

Add oil to a large sauté pan, and place over a medium heat. Brown the meat on all sides, then remove and set aside.

Add the carrots, onions, and garlic to the pan, and sauté for about 5 minutes.

Add the spices, tomato puree, and stock, and mix well.

Add the meat, vegetables, and liquid to the slow cooker, and cook on low heat for 6 hours.

Add the chickpeas and chopped fruit, and cook for another hour.

Serve with couscous (not included in recipe) and sprinkle with cilantro and almonds before serving.

Nutritional Information: per serving; not including couscous
Calories 370
Total Fat 11g
Saturated Fat 3.7g
Cholesterol 101mg
Sodium 150mg
Total Carbs 27.7g
Dietary Fiber 5.7g
Sugar 11.6g
Protein 38.8g

Additional Notes

Use this section to make additional notes.

_____

_____

_____

_____

_____

_____

_____

_____

_____

_____

_____

_____

_____

_____

PORK RECIPES

Pineapple Pork Roast

Servings: 4

Ingredients:

32 oz. boneless pork roast
1 ½ tsp. sea salt
½ tsp. ground black pepper
1 x 20 oz. can pineapple juice, in natural juices and undrained
1 cup chopped dried cranberries

Instructions:

Rub the salt and pepper over all sides of the pork, and place in the slow cooker.

Pour the pineapple chunks over the port, including the juice.

Sprinkle over the cranberries, and set the cooker to a low heat for 7 hours.

Serve with brown rice and mixed vegetables – not included in the recipe.

Nutritional Information: per serving - not including rice and/or vegetables

Calories 465kcal

Total Fat 10.7g

Saturated Fat 3.7g

Cholesterol 134.3mg

Sodium 107.2mg

Total Carbs 44.3g

Dietary Fiber 3g

Sugar 36.1g

Protein 47.4g

_____

_____

_____

_____

_____

_____

_____

_____

_____

Pork Roast or Chops

Servings: 8

Ingredients:

1 large onion, peeled and sliced
32 oz. baby carrots, full or sliced
40 oz. boneless pork roast, or 8 x 5oz. chops
1 cup hot water
¼ cup brown sugar
3 tbsp. red wine vinegar
2 tbsp. soy sauce
1 tbsp. tomato ketchup
½ tsp. black pepper
½ tsp. sea salt
¼ tsp. garlic powder
1 dash hot pepper sauce, or more to taste

Instructions:

Place the onion slices evenly at the bottom of the slow cooker.

Place the pork on top of the onions.

In a bowl, mix together the rest of the ingredients, except the baby carrots.

Pour over the pork, and then add the baby carrots.

Cook on a low heat for 6-8 hours, or on high for 3-4 hours.

Note: Delicious served with a jacket potato and green beans (not included in the recipe).

Nutritional Information: per serving - not including potato and beans

Calories 273kcal
Total Fat 9.5g
Saturated Fat 3.2g
Cholesterol 77.3mg
Sodium 402.4mg
Total Carbs 13.8g
Dietary Fiber 1.5g
Sugar 6.5g
Protein 31.6g

_____

_____

_____

_____

_____

_____

Savory Pork Chop Dinner

Servings - 2
Ingredients
2 tsp. loin pork chops, trimmed of all visible fat
¼ tbsp. extra-virgin olive oil
6 to 8 very small new potatoes, cut in small pieces
¼ tsp. garlic powder
1 tbsp. fresh sage, chopped
1 tbsp. fresh rosemary, chopped
1 tsp. ground thyme
1 x 15 oz. can of low-fat cream of mushroom soup
¼ cup white wine
¼ tsp. freshly ground black pepper
1 pinch of sea salt to taste

Instructions
Pour the oil into the slow cooker, add the onions and new potatoes.

Season with the salt, pepper, garlic powder, sage, rosemary, and thyme.

Mix so all vegetables are evenly covered with oil, herbs, and spices.

Trim all fat from chops, and wash.

Place on top of the vegetables.

In a small bowl, mix together the soup and wine until smooth. Pour mixture over the meat.

Cover and cook on low heat for a minimum of 6 hours.

Serve immediately, or keep on warm setting until needed.

Nutritional Information

Calories 425kcal

Total Fat 18.7g

Saturated Fat 6g

Cholesterol 66.7mg

Sodium 819.4mg

Total Carbs 33.2g

Dietary Fiber 4.7g

Sugar 3.7g

Protein 24.6g

_____

_____

_____

_____

_____

Pork with Greens and Beans

Servings - 8
Ingredients

Spice rub
1 tbsp. chili powder
½ tsp. red pepper flakes
½ tsp. sea salt

32 oz. pork shoulder, all fat removed
3 cloves garlic, halved
1 x 14.5 oz. can diced tomatoes (low in sodium)
2 x 14.5 oz. cans cannellini beans, drained and rinsed
2 cups kale
½ cup pumpkin seeds, shelled

Instructions
Mix the chili powder, pepper flakes, and salt together, and rub over the pork 1 hour prior to cooking (or the night before).

When ready, add the pork to the slow cooker with the garlic. Cook on low heat for 5-6 hours.

Break the meat up into chunks, and add the tomatoes, beans, and kale. Cook for another hour.

Before serving, toast the pumpkin seeds, and sprinkle over the stew.

Nutritional Information: per serving
Calories 285.9kcal
Total Fat 15.6g
Saturated Fat 5.1g
Cholesterol 72mg
Sodium 408.3mg
Total Carbs 11.7g
Dietary Fiber 3.6g
Sugar 0.2g
Protein 25.9

_____

_____

_____

_____

_____

_____

_____

_____

_____

Additional Notes

Use this section to make additional notes.

_____

_____

_____

_____

_____

_____

_____

_____

_____

_____

_____

_____

_____

_____

VEGETARIAN RECIPES

Veggie Stew

Servings: 6

Ingredients:

1 cup sweet corn
1 cup green beans
1 x 14oz. can black-eyed beans
1 cup lima beans
1 cup carrots, peeled and chopped
1 cup celery, chopped
1 medium onion, peeled and chopped
1 small can tomato puree
2 cups vegetable stock (low sodium)
2 tbsp. Worcestershire sauce
Sea salt and black pepper to season

Instructions:

Add all ingredients to the slow cooker and mix well. Cook on a low heat for 8 hours and serve immediately, or leave on the warm setting until needed.

Nutritional Information:

Calories 186kcal
Total Fat 1.2g

Saturated Fat 0.1g
Cholesterol 0mg
Sodium 692.9mg
Total Carbs 38.8g
Dietary Fiber 10.3g
Sugar 6.1g
Protein 8.3g

———————————————————

———————————————————

———————————————————

———————————————————

———————————————————

———————————————————

———————————————————

———————————————————

———————————————————

———————————————————

Vegetable Curry

Servings: 9

Ingredients:

1 tbsp. extra virgin olive oil

4 medium carrots, peeled and sliced

1 large onion, peeled and thinly sliced

3 garlic cloves, peeled and thinly sliced

2 tbsp. curry powder

1 tsp. ground cumin

½ tsp. garam masala

½ tsp. turmeric

4 - 5 medium red potatoes

8 oz. fresh or frozen green beans

3 cups canned chickpeas, drained and rinsed

2 large tomatoes, diced

½ cup frozen peas

½ cup light coconut milk

Instructions:

In a saucepan, heat the oil, and sauté the carrots and onions for about 3-4 minutes.

Add the garlic, curry powder, cumin, gram macula and turmeric, and cook for a further 2 minutes, mixing well.

Remove from the heat. Transfer to the slow cooker. and add the potatoes, beans, chickpeas, tomatoes, and vegetable stock. Stir all ingredients together.

Cook on a low heat for 5 ½ hours. Add the peas and coconut milk, and cook for a further 15 minutes before serving.

Serve on its own or with rice (not included in the recipe).

Nutritional Information: per serving - not including rice
Calories 183.6kcal
Total Fat 3.8g
Saturated Fat 1.1g
Cholesterol 0mg
Sodium 396.6mg
Total Carbs 30.5g
Dietary Fiber 8.2g
Sugar 4.9g
Protein 7g

Vegetable Chili

Servings: 8

Ingredients:

2 tsp. extra virgin olive oil

1 large onion, peeled and diced

2 stalks celery, diced

2 carrots, peeled and diced

2 cloves garlic, chopped

1 bell pepper, diced

2 tbsp. chili powder

2 tsp. ground cumin

¼ tsp. red pepper flakes

1 x 29oz. can crushed tomatoes

3 x 15.5oz. cans red kidney, drained and rinsed

12oz. butternut squash, peeled and diced

1 cup vegetable stock

Instructions:

In a medium saucepan, sauté the onions, carrots, and celery for about 4 minutes.

Add the garlic and bell pepper, stir, and sauté for a further 2 minutes.

Add the spices and cook for another minute, stirring continuously. Remove from heat.

Add the vegetables and remaining ingredients to the slow cooker and mix well.

Cook on a low heat for 6 hours. Serve immediately, on its own or with rice (not included in recipe), or leave on the warm setting until needed.

Nutritional Information:
Calories 263.4kcal
Total Fat 2.5g
Saturated Fat 0.3g
Cholesterol 0mg
Sodium 472.9mg
Total Carbs 51.4g
Dietary Fiber 18.6g
Sugar 4.6g
Protein 12.9g

_____

_____

_____

Additional Notes

Use this section to make additional notes.

_____

_____

_____

_____

_____

_____

_____

_____

_____

_____

_____

_____

_____

Additional Notes

Use this section to make additional notes.

_____

_____

_____

_____

_____

_____

_____

_____

_____

_____

_____

_____

_____

SOUP RECIPES

Good for You Potato Soup

Servings: 15 servings

Ingredients:

6 large potatoes
3 large carrots
3 stalks celery, chopped
2 onions, peeled and chopped
4 chicken stock cubes (low sodium)
6 cups water
1 can nonfat evaporated milk
½ cup shredded cheese - optional

Instructions:

Add all ingredients, except the evaporated milk, to the slow cooker, and mix together well.

Cook on low heat for 8-10 hours, or high heat for 3-4 hours.

Add evaporated milk, and allow to cook for another 10 minutes.

Serve with cheese if desired.

Nutritional Information: per serving - does not include optional cheese

Calories 136.6kcal
Total Fat 0.3g
Saturated Fat 0.1g
Cholesterol 1g
Sodium 265.6mg
Total Carbs 29.3g
Dietary Fiber 4.5g
Sugar 4.7g
Protein 4.7g

_____

_____

_____

_____

_____

_____

_____

_____

_____

_____

Stuffed Green Pepper Soup

Servings: 6

Ingredients:
32oz. lean ground beef
1 large onion, peeled and chopped
2 cups of diced tomatoes
2 cups green peppers, chopped
2 cups tomato puree
3 cups water
1 tbsp. beef bouillon (low sodium)
1 cup cooked rice, white or brown
Sea salt and pepper to season

Instructions:
In a pan, sauté the ground beef until browned.

Add the beef and all the other ingredients to the slow cooker, and cook on a low heat for 6-8 hours. Serve immediately or keep on the warm setting until needed.

Nutritional Information:
Calories 216kcal
Total Fat 5.1g
Saturated Fat 2.1g
Cholesterol 43.4g
Sodium 480.7mg

Total Carbs 21.8g
Dietary Fiber 2.5g
Sugar 5.7g
Protein 18.8g

Fiesta Black Bean Soup

Servings: 6

Ingredients

6 cups chicken stock (low sodium)

12 oz. potatoes, peeled and diced

16 oz. can black beans, drained

8 oz. ham, diced

½ onion, peeled and diced

4 oz. jalapeno peppers, sliced

2 cloves garlic, minced

2 tsp. dried oregano leaves

2 tsp. dried cilantro leaves

1 ½ tsp. dried thyme leaves

1 tsp. ground cumin

Garnish:

Sour cream, one dollop per serving

Diced green or red peppers

Instructions:

Add all the ingredients to the slow cooker, cover, and cook on a low heat for 8-10 hours, or a high heat for 4-5 hours.

Garnish, if desired, and serve.

Nutritional Information: per serving

Calories 164kcal

Total Fat 2.2g

Saturated Fat 0.5g

Cholesterol 10.8g
Sodium 899mg
Total Carbs 26g
Dietary Fiber 6.7g
Sugar 0.5g
Protein 11.8g

_____

_____

_____

_____

_____

_____

_____

_____

_____

_____

_____

_____

White Bean, Spinach, & Spicy Sausage Soup

Servings: 4

Ingredients:
1 cup white beans, soaked overnight, then rinsed and drained
2 carrots, peeled and chopped
1 medium onion, peeled and chopped
2 garlic cloves, minced
¼ tsp. black pepper
Pinch red pepper flakes
½ tsp. dried oregano
¼ tsp. dried thyme
4 cups chicken stock (low sodium)
1 cup diced tomatoes
6oz. fresh baby spinach
6oz. smoked sausage

Instructions:
Soak the beans overnight, making sure to rinse them thoroughly before you use them.

Add the beans, carrots, onion, garlic, spices, and stock to the slow cooker, and cook on a low heat for 6-8 hours, until the beans are tender.

Add about half of the soup to a blender (leave the cap off, but cover with a cloth to allow the steam to escape) puree until smooth.

Return to the cooker, and add the spinach, tomatoes, and sausage. Mix well, and cook for a further 20 minutes.

Nutritional Information:

Calories 216.5kcal
Total Fat 7.4g
Saturated Fat 2.5g
Cholesterol 26.3g
Sodium 590.5mg
Total Carbs 33.1g
Dietary Fiber 16.1g
Sugar 4.2g
Protein 18.4g

_____

_____

_____

_____

_____

_____

_____

Additional Notes

Use this section to make additional notes.

_____

_____

_____

_____

_____

_____

_____

_____

_____

_____

_____

_____

_____

DESERT RECIPES

Spiced Apple Dessert

Servings: 8

Ingredients:
8 apples - peeled, cored, and sliced
4 tbsp. honey
4 tbsp. butter
½ tsp. cinnamon
¼ tsp. cloves

Instructions:
Place your apples in the bottom of the slow cooker, and sprinkle with the spices.

Drizzles over the honey, slice the butter, and spread evenly among the apples.

Cook on a low heat for 3-4 hours, until the apples are tender, but not pureed.

Nutritional Information:
Calories 141.5kcal
Total Fat 2.7g
Saturated Fat 0.9g
Cholesterol 0g
Sodium 42.5mg
Total Carbs 29.6g
Dietary Fiber 3.8g
Sugar 21.3g
Protein 0.2g

White Chocolate and Apricot Bread and Butter Pudding

Servings: 6

1 ½ cups half-fat cream
6oz. white chocolate baking squares, chopped coarsely
⅓ cup dried apricots, chopped
2 eggs
½ cup light brown sugar
½ tsp. ground cardamom
3 cups bread, torn into mouth-sized chunks
¼ cup sliced almonds
1 cup warm water
Fresh raspberries – optional
Fresh grated white chocolate – optional

Ingredients:

Heat the cream in a saucepan, until very warm but not boiling. Remove from heat, and add white chocolate.

Stir until the chocolate is melted, and then add the apricots, mixing well.

In a large bowl, beat the eggs with a fork, and whisk in the sugar and cardamom.

Mix in the chocolate mixture, and gently stir in the bread and almonds.

Add the mixture to a soufflé dish or similar dish (making sure it will fit inside your slow cooker).

Cover the dish tightly with foil. Make a strip that is long enough to go underneath the dish and up the sides, which you can use to lift the dish out of the cooker once it is cooked.

Pour the warm water around the soufflé dish and cook on a low heat for 4 hours, or a high heat for 2 hours.

Remove from the cooker, and serve in individual dishes with the optional raspberries and chocolate.

Nutritional Information: per serving - (doesn't include raspberries or chocolate
Calories 345kcal
Total Fat 17g
Saturated Fat 8g
Cholesterol 98g
Sodium 191mg
Total Carbs 42g
Dietary Fiber 2g
Sugar 35g
Protein 8g

Coconut Mocha Poached Pears

Servings: 8

Ingredients
6 medium ripe pears (should still be firm to touch)
¼ cup light brown sugar
2 tbsp. unsweetened cocoa powder
⅔ cup unsweetened coconut milk
⅓ cup strong coffee
Light cream to serve (optional)
Toasted coconut to serve (optional)
Grated chocolate to serve (optional)

Instructions:
Peel the pears, then quarter lengthwise, and remove cores.

Place the pears in the bottom of the slow cooker.

In a bowl, stir together the sugar and cocoa powder. Add the coconut milk and coffee, and mix together well. Pour over the pears in the slow cooker.

Cover and cook on a low heat for 3½-4 hours, or until pears are tender.

Serve in individual bowls with the optional topping about.

Nutritional Information: per serving - does not include any optional toppings

Calories 125kcal
Total Fat 1g
Saturated Fat 1g
Cholesterol 0g
Sodium 7mg ,
Total Carbs 29g
Dietary Fiber 4g
Sugar 21g
Protein 0g

_____

_____

_____

_____

_____

_____

_____

_____

_____

Lemon Berry Pudding Slow Cooker Cake

Servings: 6

Ingredients:

3 eggs
1 cup fresh blueberries and/or fresh raspberries
1 tbsp. light brown sugar
½ cup light brown sugar
¼ cup all-purpose flour
2 tsp. finely grated lemon peel
¼ tsp. sale
1 cup fat-free milk
3 tbsp. lemon juice
3 tbsp. butter, melted

Instructions:

Coat the slow cooker with oil.

Place the berries in the bottom of the cooker, and sprinkle with the 1 tbsp. of light brown sugar.

Separate the eggs into a bowl.

In another bowl, combine the ½ cup of sugar with the flour, lemon peel, and salt. Mix together well.

Add the milk, lemon juice, melted butter, and the egg yolks. Beat with an electric mixer (or by hand) until well combined.

Wash mixer and in another bowl, use to whisk the egg whites into soft peaks.

Fo3ld the whites into the batter mix, and then pour over the berries, spreading evenly.

Cook on a low-heat setting for 2½-3 hours. Remove crockery liner (if possible), and allow to cool for 1 hour on a wire rack (leave lid on).

Nutritional Information:
Calories 200kcal
Total Fat 7g
Saturated Fat 2g
Cholesterol 107g
Sodium 187mg
Total Carbs 29g
Dietary Fiber 1g
Sugar 24g
Protein 5g

Additional Notes

Use this section to make additional notes.

_____

_____

_____

_____

_____

_____

_____

_____

_____

_____

_____

_____

_____

CONCLUSION

Slow cooking is undoubtedly a lifesaver for the busy mom who wants to ensure her family has a nutritious and delicious meal at the end of the day.

Families tend to come and go at different times, and having the ability to leave food "warming" so that family members can go to it when they need it is perfect. No more worrying that kids will dip into fast and "convenient" foods that are not necessarily good for them.

The DASH diet is so easy and straight forward to follow. Combining it with slow cooking could not be any simpler. None of the recipes here take longer than 15 minutes to prepare, and all can be done ahead of time. Prepare them the night before, and leave them in the fridge. Then all you have to do is pop it on in the morning before you head out for your day, and it is done. It really is a match made in heaven.

Taking the time to incorporate the principles of the DASH diet into your lifestyle, on a permanent basis, is a worthwhile effort. Be sure and check out the rest of the recipe collections in the *DASH Diet Cookbook* series.

Yes, You've Done It!

Congratulations! You've made it to the end of this cookbook. I hope this is only the beginning of an adventure for you into a whole new lifestyle with an emphasis on clean eating and a healthy lifestyle.

Get Your Free copy of DASH Diet Tips, Strategies, and Success Stories now.

GET YOUR FREE
DASH DIET BONUS
DASH Diet Tips, Strategies, and Success Stories

Go to: www.MyDashDietCookbooks.com

My DASH Diet Cookbook Series:

DASH DIET EASY SLOW COOKER
CROCK POT RECIPES

30+ mouthwatering recipes that will save you time. These good clean eating, delicious, quick and easy slow—cooker recipes are gluten—free and dairy-free. You'll find recipes for breakfast, dinner, soups and stews, and dessert recipes, all for one—pot slow cooking.

DASH DIET RECIPES for VEGANS

Looking for DASH Diet recipes Vegan-style? While lean meat is allowed on the standard DASH diet, this recipe collection focuses on recipes designed for vegans who wish to give the diet a try. Vegans and vegetarians want to modify the DASH diet, so this collection helps them make that transition. You'll find plenty of tips to help.

DASH DIET QUICK & EASY RECIPES for BREAKFAST, LUNCH, & SNACKS

Inside this collection, you'll find easy and tasty meals that you can enjoy while on the DASH Diet. No need for guess work.

DASH DIET QUICK & EASY RECIPES
SOUPS, SALADS, STIR FRY & SPRING ROLES

Looking for light and easy recipes that incorporate the DASH diet plan? This collection focuses on just that. Inside you'll find recipes like Ginger Veggie Spring Rolls, Asian Veggie Salad with Snow Peas, Shrimp and Tomato Stir-Fry, and even Tuscan White Bean Vegetable Soup and so much more.

About the Author

Like my DASH Diet Smoothies and Recipes page.
www.facebook.com/DASH Diet Smoothies and
Recipes

Robertina Whelans first learned of the DASH Diet
when she was diagnosed with hypertension and found
it to be an effective way to lower her blood pressure.
Today, she seeks to share what she's learned about the
DASH Diet with others so they, too, can reap similar
rewards

Follow my Amazon Author Page
amazon.com/author/RobertinaWhelans

Enjoyed this Cookbook?

I hope you've enjoyed this collection of smoothie recipes and hope you let others know about the DASH Diet, its benefits, and my DASH Diet cookbook series. Like every other author, I do my best to put together a book that my readers will enjoy and find helpful.

One feature you may enjoy more and more as time goes by are the blank lined pages in the paperback editions.

Also, your feedback is crucial to the success of authors like me who are helped by the readers who have read, enjoyed, and found their books useful or helpful, and who are then happy to let others know. If you have enjoyed this book, I'd be grateful if you would take a few minutes to leave an honest review on Amazon or wherever you either bought the book or wherever you enjoy sharing your reading experiences.

Thank you!

Robertina Whelans

NOTES

_____

_____

_____

_____

_____

_____

_____

_____

_____

INDEX

61061795R00073

Made in the USA
Middletown, DE
06 January 2018